Baker

by **Dana Meachen Rau**

Reading Consultant: Nanci R. Vargus, Ed.D.

Marshall Cavendish
Benchmark
New York

Picture Words

 bagels

 baker

 bread

 cakes

cookies

 doughnuts

 muffins

 pies

A 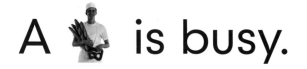 is busy.

A makes .

A  makes .

A  makes .

A makes .

A  makes .

A  makes .

16

A  makes .

18

A  makes you smile.

Words to Know

busy (BIZ-ee)
    to have a lot to do

smile
    a happy look on your face

Find Out More

Books

Bull, Jane. *The Baking Book*. New York: DK Publishing Inc., 2005.

Dunnington, Rose. *The Greatest Cookies Ever*. Asheville, NC: Lark Books, 2005.

Lewis, Sara. *Kids' Baking: Over 60 Delicious Recipes for Children to Make*. New York: Sterling Publishing Company, Inc., 2006.

Pillsbury. *Pillsbury Kids Cookbook: Food Fun for Boys and Girls*. Hoboken, NJ: John Wiley & Sons, Inc., 2005.

Videos

My First Cooking Video: A Kids' Guide to Making Fun Things to Eat. Sony Kids' Video.

Web Sites

Betty Crocker: Kid Friendly Baking
www.bettycrocker.com/How-To/Baking-Basics/ Baking-Strategies/kid-friendly-baking.htm

Cooking With Kids
www.cookingwithkids.com

About the Author

Dana Meachen Rau is an author, editor, and illustrator. A graduate of Trinity College in Hartford, Connecticut, she has written more than two hundred books for children, including nonfiction, biographies, early readers, and historical fiction. She likes to bake cookies with her family in Burlington, Connecticut.

About the Reading Consultant

Nanci R. Vargus, Ed.D., wants all children to enjoy reading. She used to teach first grade. Now she works at the University of Indianapolis. Nanci helps young people become teachers. She and her granddaughters Charlotte, Corinne, and Adara decorate a gingerbread house each Christmas.

Marshall Cavendish Benchmark
99 White Plains Road
Tarrytown, NY 10591-9001
www.marshallcavendish.us

All Internet addresses were correct at the time of printing.

Library of Congress Cataloging-in-Publication Data

Rau, Dana Meachen, 1971–
Baker / by Dana Meachen Rau.
    p. cm. — (Benchmark rebus)
Summary: "Easy to read text with rebuses explores the many varieties of treats found in a bakery"—Provided by publisher.
Includes bibliographical references.
ISBN 978-0-7614-2623-3
1. Baking—Juvenile literature. 2. Baked products—Juvenile literature. 3. Bakeries—Juvenile literature. 4. Vocabulary—Juvenile literature. 5. Rebuses—Juvenile literature. I. Title. II. Series.
TX683.R38 2007
641.8'15—dc22
        2007002896

Editor: Christine Florie
Publisher: Michelle Bisson
Art Director: Anahid Hamparian
Series Designer: Virginia Pope

Photo research by Connie Gardner

Rebus images, with the exception of Baker, provided courtesy of *Dorling Kindersley.*

Cover photo by Peter Beck/CORBIS

The photographs in this book are used with permission and through the courtesy of:
SuperStock: p. 2 Mauritius (Baker); *Alamy Images*: p. 5 Peter Jordan; p. 7 JCB-People; *SuperStock*: p. 9 age footstock; *PhotoEdit*: p. 11 Mark Richards; p. 17 Michael Newman; p. 19 David Young Wolff; *Corbis*: p. 13 Steve Prezant; p. 15 Ed Quinn; p. 21 Michael Pole.

Printed in Malaysia
1 3 5 6 4 2